Travel and Tourism

The Insider Career Guides is a dynamic series of books designed to give you the inside track on individual careers – how to get in, how to get on, even how to get out.

Based on the real-life experiences of people actually working in these fields, each title offers a combination of hard practical information and insider information on working culture, the pros and cons of different areas of work, prospects for promotion, etc.

Other titles in the series:

Banking and the City
Karen Holmes

The Environment
Melanie Allen

Information and Communications Technology
Jacquetta Megarry

Retailing
Liz Edwards

Sport
Robin Hardwick

About the Series Editor
Following a successful career as a teacher and lecturer in the UK and the Far East, Karen Holmes now works as a freelance writer, editor and project manager. Specialising in learning and careers, she has authored a range of careers literature for publishers and other commercial organisations.

Travel and Tourism

by

Karen France

First published in 1999 by
The Industrial Society
Robert Hyde House
48 Bryanston Square
London W1H 7LN

© The Industrial Society 1999

ISBN 1 85835 598 2

British Library Cataloguing-in-Publication Data.
A catalogue record for this book is available from the
British Library.

Typeset by: The Midlands Book Typesetting Company
Printed by: Cromwell Press
Cover by: Sign Design
Cover image by: Tony Stone

The Industrial Society is a Registered Charity No. 290003

CONTENTS

Introduction	**vii**
Part One – The Job	**1**
Travel and tourism in Britain	5
So what's in it for you?	7
Selling holidays and travel	8
Transporting holidaymakers to their destination	13
Providing accommodation and services at the destination	18
Vital statistics	25
Part Two – The Person	**29**
Marketing yourself	32
Getting advice	33
What do you want?	34
Just for fun...	36
What are employers looking for?	41
Part Three – Getting in, Getting on... Getting out	**47**
Getting in	50
The Insider guide to completing application forms	52
The Insider guide to writing effective CVs	53
The Insider guide to writing effective covering letters	54
The Insider guide to performing well at interviews	55
The Insider guide to performing well at assessment centres	57
Work experience	58
Getting in as a non-graduate	59

Getting in as a graduate   61
Getting on   62
Getting out   65

Jargon buster   **67**

Want to find out more?   **69**

Want to read all about it?   **73**

INTRODUCTION

You enjoy working with people, you have endless amounts of patience, your communication skills are second to none and you love to travel.

Working in travel and tourism seems like the ideal career choice for you – but is it? How can you find out what the industry is about, what sorts of jobs it offers and whether you have the right skills and attributes to succeed?

You can contact organisations that work in the industry, look at recruitment literature, surf the Internet for tour operators' websites or talk to the professionals, the people who already work there. Or you can read this book where a lot of the hard work has already been done for you.

The *Insider Career Guides* give you the inside story on what it is really like to work in a particular field of employment. These titles will help you find out more about different professions and their cultures, day-to-day working routines and the opportunities that exist for you.

In this book, *The Insider Career Guide to Travel and Tourism*, you will find useful information about:

- trends within the travel and tourism industry
- how to start your career
- what employers are looking for in new recruits
- opportunities for training and development
- promotion and the way to the top.

The book is divided into three sections.

Part One, *The Job*, gives you an up-to-date overview of the travel and tourism industry, including:

- the various sectors of the industry and what they actually do

- brief descriptions of individual areas of employment within these industry sectors
- recruitment trends
- an insight into the daily routine of some of the people who work in travel and tourism
- the 'vital statistics' – important details such as the levels of salary and types of benefits you can expect to earn.

Part Two, *The Person*, focuses on some of the people who work in the industry.

Starting with a simple quiz that helps you assess whether you have the qualities and skills to succeed in the world of travel and tourism, it goes on to look at:

- the skills and experience required of successful recruits
- the personal characteristics that will help you succeed in the job
- information from industry insiders about their working lives.

Part Three, *Getting in, Getting on... Getting out*, looks at:

- where you can find out about current vacancies
- how to make applications that catch the eye of company recruiters
- the training and development you will receive once you work in travel and tourism
- opportunities for promotion and advancement
- related careers – where do people who leave the industry go next?

No book can tell you everything you want to know about a particular career or industry. Travel and tourism offers many different opportunities, and when you have read *The Insider Career Guide to Travel and Tourism*, you will probably want to carry out your own research.

To help you, we have included useful contact and website addresses so you can access more information.

With checklists to help you plan your job search, case studies, quotes from industry professionals and 'myth busters' that address popular misconceptions about working life, you'll find plenty of inside information in these pages to start you on your chosen career.

part one | the job

the job

Introduction

Travel and tourism is already big business and the good news for jobseekers is that its growth is set to continue (anticipated annual growth worldwide is 6%). The largest tour operators in the United Kingdom have turnovers in excess of £1 billion and employ thousands of staff. In the last ten years, this country has seen a 30% increase in the numbers of people employed in the travel and tourism industry. Every year, around 1,000 people are recruited into high street travel agencies and hundreds more are employed to work in resorts all over the world.

There are a number of economic and social factors that are contributing to this growth. An increasing number of people have higher disposable incomes and are able to take more than one holiday a year. The cost of travelling is not prohibitively high and improved transport systems have made journeys faster and easier... Only 40 years ago, going further than Blackpool or Bournemouth for a week's holiday in the summer would have been far beyond the aspirations of the average British worker. Now, a couple of weeks' holiday in Spain, the Greek Islands or Gran Canaria is much more accessible.

Changing trends

The travel and tourism industry is constantly changing and evolving to keep pace with the needs of its customers. One good example of this is the growth of specialist holiday companies. Travellers are becoming more experienced and discerning, with many people choosing to travel independently, seeking activity holidays or wanting to travel further afield to more exotic destinations. The travel industry has had to become more diverse to cope with these demands. Instead of simply providing package holidays for the mass market, it is tailoring its services to meet the needs of tourists who want something different. Alongside the established high street travel agencies, there is a growing army of companies which cater for the independent traveller. They offer tailor-made programmes or simply act as booking agents for flights and accommodation. There are now specialist holiday companies who offer anything from New Age therapy breaks in Skiathos to 'extreme skiing' in Canada or tours of Alaska for the over-55s. Whatever you want to do (as long as it's legal!), there will be a specialist travel agency to help you do it.

Another noticeable trend, tied to the increase in disposable income, is the popularity of short breaks both in this country and overseas. People work hard and feel the need to enjoy their leisure time. Many of us take more than one holiday a year, with a trip overseas in the summer and a number of three- or four-day mini-holidays throughout the rest of the year. These may be to holiday villages in this country, a city break to Paris or Amsterdam or simply a couple of nights away from it all in a country pub. It all creates work for the companies that make the bookings and provide the transport and accommodation.

Business travel is another area of growth. Every day, four million business travellers take to the air. With their mobile offices (mobile phones, laptop computers and modems) they can seek new markets and business opportunities anywhere in the world. Business travellers represent a highly lucrative market for the travel and tourism industry. Airlines and transport companies rely heavily on this sector to fill their more expensive business and first-class seats. Hotels, particularly those in city centres, have been quick to take advantage of the need both for comfortable rooms and for conference facilities.

Infrastructure changes

Travel and tourism are big business and they have a knock-on effect in generating growth in other industries. Across the world, travellers and holidaymakers are demanding higher standards of service, value for money and greater comfort. Both travel companies and governments can see the advantages of investing in infrastructure improvements to make travel as stress-free as possible. For example, the new train link from Paddington to Heathrow Airport cuts the journey time down to a mere 15 minutes. Airlines are refitting their aircraft to make long-haul flights more comfortable and less of an ordeal for economy-class travellers. Hong Kong's new airport may have taken some of the excitement out of landing (pilots no longer have to weave a path through the skyscrapers), but it is now possible to travel from Chek Lap Kok airport to downtown Kowloon in only 23 minutes.

Projects such as these create thousands of jobs in construction and service industries – and, of course, within the travel and tourism industry itself.

MYTH BUSTER

The travel industry won't expand much further

Despite huge investment in the industry and evidence that many more people are choosing to travel, only 7% of the world's population consider themselves to be tourists or travellers. This means that 93% of the world's population have yet to get started! That suggests that potential for growth is almost unlimited.

Travel and tourism in Britain

Britain has a lot to offer tourists. It has beautiful countryside, interesting cities and a wealth of history and tradition that prove irresistible to overseas visitors. There is a huge range of tourist attractions – from York Minster to the shops on Oxford Street. Of course, the British weather can prove a drawback, but we have learned to cope with that by creating more all-weather facilities.

In recent years, British fashion and style have drawn thousands of visitors from the Asia Pacific region, the Middle East, Africa and South America. Most people who come here perceive the country as safe and welcoming, and they enjoy the distinctive way of life.

In the past, the British travel and tourism industry has suffered from image problems. Poor standards of service presented a major problem (yes, *Fawlty Towers* was a mythical hotel, but a lot of people felt they had stayed somewhere similar), as did a creaking transport infrastructure that made journeys difficult, expensive and time-consuming.

Because the industry is so diverse, there will always be problems in achieving consistency of standards, but the British Tourist Authority is trying to address some of the major problems by creating better training programmes for staff in the industry and getting the industry and educators to work together to develop the skills needed to maintain a successful tourist industry.

Massive improvements have already been made. Different sectors of the travel and tourism industry have invested in customer service training programmes to upgrade skills. Accommodation standards have improved at all levels, from five-star hotels to bed and breakfast establishments, thanks to more stringent monitoring of facilities and grading systems. The reputation of food in Britain is also improving. London is acknowledged as one of the gastronomic capitals of the world. Investment in provincial centres such as Manchester and Leeds have changed their image. No longer perceived as gritty northern cities, they now boast some of the most fashionable restaurants and night life in the country. All of which should encourage still more visitors to spend their holidays (and their money) in this country.

In Britain, the travel and tourism industry is already the country's most important invisible export. More than 200,000 organisations, ranging from small businesses to multimillion pound plcs, make up the industry. All the indications are that, by the millennium, travel and tourism will be Britain's largest industry. At the moment, this country is fifth in the world's travel and tourism league.

Did you know...?

- In 1996, Europe was the fastest growing region in the world for travellers to Britain, with both revenue and visitor numbers up 12%.
- Revenue from German visitors amounted to more than £1 billion.
- Revenue from Eastern European visitors continued to grow significantly. Nearly all the main markets in this area increased their contribution to British revenue by at least 20%.
- Increased British Tourist Authority presence in the Nordic region helped to make this one of the most profitable sources of visitors to Britain from Europe.[1]

So what's in it for you?

Look at the facts again:

- There is an increase in leisure time, wealth and life expectancy (people are travelling later in life).
- Both domestic and overseas tourists are taking more trips in the form of short breaks and additional holidays.
- Visitors are being attracted from new markets, such as Eastern Europe and the Far East.
- Both central and local government are now committed to enhancing the image of the industry, providing sources of funding to help with redevelopment and training.

The future for the travel and tourism industry looks bright and the prospects for growth are excellent. That makes it a great area to consider for a career. In 1997, the travel and tourism industry employed 7% of the workforce in Britain, and it is currently responsible for one in five of all new jobs that are created.

This *Insider Career Guide* looks at some of the jobs and the people involved in the travel and tourism industry. Because the industry is so large and diverse, it is not possible to provide more than a 'sample' of some areas of

[1] *Source:* British Tourist Authority Annual Report, 1997

employment. We have divided these into three sections related to the main activities of travel and tourism organisations:

- selling holidays and travel
- transporting holidaymakers to their destination
- providing accommodation and services at the destination.

SELLING HOLIDAYS AND TRAVEL

Any potential traveller or holidaymaker has a number of decisions to make:

- Where do I want to go to?
- How do I want to get there?
- What do I want to do when I reach my destination?

Customers are becoming much more knowledgeable about travel and, consequently, their expectations are increasing. They expect high-quality standards of service, starting with the person who makes their travel arrangements. If they do not get the service they anticipate, they will vote with their feet and book their next holiday with another travel company.

'When I'm planning to go on holiday, there are a lot of factors that contribute to my decision as to which holiday I book. Obviously, these include getting value for money and finding a destination that will give me the sort of holiday I want. I also want a travel agent who will take an interest in my plans and who puts a lot of effort into helping me. Making the booking is part of the holiday experience so I want it to be special, not like a trip to the supermarket.'

Publishing executive

Travel agents

The starting point for most holidaymakers is the local travel agency, a shop which sells holidays on behalf of tour operators. In general, high street travel agencies cater for traditional package holidays, offering breaks to Europe or further afield, winter sun and skiing, cruises and fly-drives. They carry supplies of brochures from tour operators and will often entice customers into the shop by offering special deals or bargain holidays in their windows. Bookings are made via computer links with the tour operators and by telephone. The travel agent acts as the frontline sales person and provides all the liaison between the customer and tour operator. Travel agents can also book flights or accommodation for independent travellers, answer questions about specific destinations and provide a foreign exchange service.

Travel agencies vary in size. Some high streets will have local shops that are independently owned or part of a small chain. Others will belong to a much bigger organisation. Going Places, for example, is part of Airtours plc, a 'vertically integrated' organisation which owns travel agencies, an airline and tour operators.

Some customers bypass the travel agents and go direct to the tour operators by contacting them through advertisements in the press. Pick up any Sunday newspaper and you will see dozens of advertisements for both mainstream and specialist holidays. Brochures are sent direct to the customer and booking can be done over the phone.

Modern technology is having a strong impact on the way in which holidays are sold. Ceefax and Teletext carry information about a range of offers, particularly late availability breaks. The Internet offers a one-stop shop where customers can access the latest offers, book and pay by credit card, all without leaving their own home. Some tour company websites are so sophisticated that they can even give you a virtual guided tour of your hotel room.

Jobs in travel agencies revolve around selling and include:

- travel advisers/consultants
- foreign exchange staff
- assistant managers
- branch or area managers.

'Our travel consultants greet the customers, try to find out exactly what they are looking for and then match their needs by showing them brochures that might be of interest. They check the availability of holidays or travel, make the booking and collect the payment. When the tickets have been issued, they'll make sure the customer gets them in time. Of course, there are also general office duties as well – paperwork and keeping the place clean, tidy and welcoming.'

Assistant manager, travel agency

Travel agency staff are usually office based. Holidays are booked through computerised systems so they must be computer literate. They also need good standards of numeracy and literacy to complete booking forms and cope with the general form-filling.

Providing good standards of service is obviously key to a travel agency's success, so staff need the necessary skills to cope with customers' demands. That means:

- genuinely enjoying working with people (both customers and colleagues)
- being calm and polite even when under pressure. Small travel agencies can be very busy places
- having a good telephone manner since this will be the basis of a lot of contact with both customers and tour operators.

A day in the life...

A typical day starts at 8.45am, when I open the post and have a cup of tea. Next, I make sure that all of the foreign currency has arrived (this is ordered one day in advance). The rest of the day is a mixture. I chase enquiries, make sure brochures are ordered, up to date, stamped and on the shelf. I check that the late offers are correct and look at the e-mails sent by head office – that's how they let us know about special offers. I also chase up overdue balances from customers, and tickets and booking confirmations from tour operators. All of this is carried out in between serving people. All the data from the tour operators is on screen so I'm working on a computer a lot of the time. My day ends at 5.30pm. I work five days a week which includes Saturdays.

A lot of my time is spent dealing directly with the customers, either face to face or on the phone. The part I enjoy the most is finding the right holiday for them. The more complicated their demands, the better! There can be a lot of pressure – we're a small office with only four staff and we are constantly busy. Staying calm and not getting wound up when things go wrong is essential.

What I like least about my job is dealing with complaints. I used to take complaints personally, but now I'm better at dealing with them. People complain about the strangest things – one woman was irate because the pillowcases on her hotel bed did not match the duvet cover!

Assistant branch manager, travel agency

As most travel agency staff are constantly in view of the public, a high premium is placed on looking smart and professional at all times. Some organisations provide uniforms; all organisations expect their staff to be well-groomed. Some specialist agencies, such as those dealing with student and independent travel, may take a less formal approach.

Within the larger chains of travel agencies there will be opportunities at head office in management functions, such as training, human resource management, finance, information technology, marketing and sales, as well as administrative and clerical roles. For head office specialist functions you may need a degree, although the travel and tourism industry has a good record for promoting from within and giving people a chance to work their way up from junior roles to senior management.

Travel agencies that are part of large groups (that include tour operators and airlines) may offer opportunities to transfer across different sectors, giving staff the chance to gather experience and work in many different areas of the industry.

'We look for recruits who are happy working as sales staff and enjoy taking a customer service role – and that's not always as easy as it sounds. You need a lot of patience and tact and you need to understand people so you can tell what they really want even if they are not sure themselves! Age isn't as important as good organisational and communication skills, and if you are computer literate, that's a big plus. Much of the work is fairly routine – some people like that aspect but I guess it doesn't suit everyone.'

Recruitment manager, travel agency

Tour operators

Tour operators provide holidays and, although they may vary in size, most of them offer the same services by putting together transport, accommodation and resort facilities. They will also have a sales facility which liaises with travel agents or directly with the public.

These companies provide the staff who look after holidaymakers when they reach their destination, such as resort representatives, managers and entertainment staff. Some large-scale tour operators are part of groups which have their own airlines and hotels, so they may employ administrators and management staff to run these companies.

Depending on the size of the company, a tour operator can offer a range of jobs. As with travel agencies, some tour operators will have a large head office and offer management careers in finance, IT, customer care, marketing and sales, public relations and human resource management. For a head office post, you will usually need either a degree or a proven track record working within the travel industry. If you get a seasonal job in a resort and show aptitude, the company will try to retain your services, either by moving you to other resorts when the season ends or by finding a role for you in its offices at home.

Reservations/sales staff and administrators

Reservations staff work over the phone, booking holidays, flights and accommodation. Like travel agents, their systems are computerised so they need keyboard skills. Good communication skills are also a must since staff deal with both travel agents and the general public. Administrators issue tickets, compile flight lists and take care of the general office work. For any of these jobs, previous experience in the travel industry or experience in sales and customer service in other industries is desirable. Since reservations offices are often open long hours, staff may be asked to work shifts.

'I work for a UK tour operator, taking bookings over the phone for holiday cottages. We work a regular shift pattern across three and a half days. I'm talking directly to customers all the time and trying to match up their demands with our vacancies.

My biggest problem when I started was that I spent too long talking to people – I'd get really interested in what they were doing or they would pour out their troubles and explain they needed a holiday because their fiancé had just dumped them and they had to get away. My team leader very tactfully pointed out that psychotherapy wasn't my job but getting sales was. The computer showed that I spent nearly ten minutes talking to each customer when I should only have been averaging four and a half minutes.

The job demands that you concentrate on getting the bookings. The more calls you take, the less time you spend in conversation, and the more effective you are as a salesperson.'

Telesales, tour operator

Depending on the type of company, specialist knowledge could be needed. These advertisements give some indication of the skills operators (in this case, a tour operator specialising in skiing holidays) are looking for:

A leading ski specialist travel agency is looking for a sales consultant. A wide knowledge of the Alps is essential and ski tour operator background preferred. Age 24+. Salary according to experience.

•••

Assistants are required from October to March for the busy administration department. Applicants must be organised and numerate and a knowledge of skiing would be an advantage. French and Italian needed for one of the posts. Age 21+. Salary according to age and experience.

At interview, candidates will be asked for evidence to prove their skills in these areas. As with many jobs in the travel and tourism industry, languages are definitely an advantage. At interview (or over the phone prior to interview) applicants can expect an oral test to make sure they meet the required language levels.

The holiday industry has peaks and troughs, so tour operators may take staff on seasonally. Spending a period of time as a temporary worker in reservations or sales is a good way both to get your foot in the door of a particular company and to find out if you are suited to the industry.

TRANSPORTING HOLIDAYMAKERS TO THEIR DESTINATION

Customers have to make decisions about how they will get to their chosen destination. Air travel is increasingly popular especially for long journeys – in 1997, nearly 57 million travellers passed through Heathrow Airport. But there are other options, including travelling by sea (usually on a cruise), by rail or by bus.

Getting people from A to B is an enormous industry in itself. Thousands of staff work at airports and ports. Some of these will be employed by the operating companies that own and administer the premises; others will be employed by companies which work from the premises, such as airlines and tour operators.

Airport staff

By far the majority of employees in an airport operating company will work for the customer services department. Their job is to help people who are travelling by providing information and assistance.

'The purpose of my job is to be able to help people and to answer any questions they may have. This could include enquiries about flights or meeting people from flights. The information desk is open 24 hours a day so I work shifts. The first thing I do when I take over from my colleagues is to find out any essential information, such as flight cancellations or delays. We also have a message board for passengers. For instance, if someone has phoned to say that they cannot meet a passenger as arranged, we will make sure the passenger is tannoyed as soon as the flight arrives so that we can pass on the message. We have access to a computerised flight control system which tells us everything we need to know about the flights.

We work two-hour shifts in the TV room inputting information that shows on all the public display monitors. Passengers use the monitors to find out when they should move to the departure gates.

To be successful in this job, you need good customer service skills, so experience of working with the public is useful. Languages are also useful. I speak Urdu, Punjabi and Hindi. I would recommend anyone who wants to work in the travel and tourism industry to improve their language skills. Although languages are not always required for a job, they are definitely an asset.'

Information desk assistant

Tour operators also have their own staff working out of the airport. They greet customers, help them check in if necessary and generally ensure that departure proceeds smoothly.

Passenger service agents

Passenger service agents are the people who help travellers to pass quickly and easily through airports. Using a computerised system they check in passengers, issue boarding cards and pass baggage over to the airline. They will then escort passengers to and from aircraft both on arrival and departure.

Passenger service agents are employed by handling agents, companies in airports that are responsible for checking in passengers, processing baggage, despatching and cleaning aircraft, and freight operations.

Airline staff

Many jobs in the travel industry, such as cabin crew or couriers, are perceived as being glamorous. Anyone employed in these roles knows it is very hard work involving long hours with heavy demands on your stamina, tact and patience. It can even be dangerous if you are faced with an unruly or violent passenger. Nevertheless, working for an airline remains an attractive career proposition for thousands of hopeful applicants so it's an area worth looking at more closely.

Cabin crew

The image of the immaculately groomed, smiling cabin crew member who jets off at regular intervals to stopover in New York, Sydney or Rio prevails. Some of them do. Many more spend their days (or nights) shuttling between Birmingham or London and Malaga.

> 'You'd certainly be very lucky if you finished your training and were immediately put on a flight to some glamorous location. Like any other job, you work your way through the ranks so you start off with the more mundane work.'
>
> Cabin crew attendant

Cabin crew are employed to carry out a number of functions, the most important of which is maintaining the safety of passengers. As a traveller you may pay scant regard to the steward who is going through the safety routine at the front of the cabin, but that is one of their primary roles – to make sure that everyone on the aircraft is aware of the safety procedures. They also serve meals and drinks, sell duty-free goods and generally make sure that passengers are comfortable on board the aircraft. All of which sounds fairly straightforward, until you consider that there may be hundreds of people on the aircraft who have to be served in relatively short periods of time, the turbulence might be so bad that you can hardly stand up and one of your jobs is periodically cleaning the toilets!

> 'I love my job, but there's no denying that it is hard work. If a passenger doesn't enjoy the flight, gets scared or simply a bit bored and frustrated with the journey, they can't just get off and go somewhere else. We have to help them and to deal with their problems as soon as they arise. Physically it is very taxing. You are on your feet for long periods of time and, as any long-haul passenger knows, altitude plays havoc with your ankles, your hair and your general sense of well-being.'
>
> *Cabin crew attendant*

Cabin crew work in teams so they need to be flexible. Like the passengers, cabin crew can't get off the plane in mid-flight if they are unhappy or have had a disagreement with a colleague. This is a job that demands a high degree of maturity as well as good communication and 'people' skills.

Cabin crew are generally required to live within a maximum of one hour's travelling time from the airport. They definitely do not work nine to five, so clearly anyone looking for a job with regular hours should not apply. For those staff who get on to long-haul flights, there may be considerable periods of time spent away from home.

Airlines have their own person specification for cabin crew, but typically they will look for someone who:

- is within the 20–35 age bracket
- has a minimum of four GCSEs
- has good numeracy, literacy and language skills
- can swim at least 30 metres.

For safety rather than aesthetic reasons, airlines are very specific about the physical attributes of their cabin crew. Most airlines specify height restrictions – 5ft 2ins to 6ft 2ins is typical – and weight must be in proportion to height.

Applicants must have normal vision (contact lenses are acceptable), no visible scars or tattoos and clear diction. A high standard of personal presentation is essential.

'People who succeed as cabin crew are bright, cheerful, patient, approachable, tactful and good listeners. They are also willing to muck in and handle the more unpleasant parts of the job cheerfully. It also helps if they like flying. You would be amazed how many applications we get from people who have never been on an aircraft and who discover the first time they take to the skies that they are petrified!'

Cabin crew attendant

Pilot

The path to becoming a commercial pilot is not easy. It is highly competitive, fantastically expensive, full of obstacles and extremely demanding. It will take you years to qualify and then you will be in competition with other equally competent people for very few jobs. Still interested? Then your next step should be to have at least one trial lesson to find out if you have the nerve, motor skills and aptitude to make the grade as a pilot.

Anyone considering a career as a pilot must have good academic qualifications, particularly in Science, Mathematics, Geography and Technology – a minimum of five GCSEs (grade C or above) and at least two A level passes or equivalent. They must also be physically fit.

There are three main routes to becoming a commercial pilot.

1. You can join the armed forces. The Royal Air Force, Army or Navy provide first-class training, but it is difficult to get in and a military environment does not suit everyone.
2. Some airlines provide sponsorship, but getting on to these schemes is difficult. You will need to have completed basic training and gained a Private Pilot's Licence before you start and you will be tied to the airline for a number of years after you qualify to make sure you 'work off' the cost of your training.

3. Independently, you can obtain a Private Pilot's Licence and gain experience either as an instructor or as a general aviator. This route could easily cost in excess of £30,000 and there is no guarantee of a job at the end. The quickest way to gain these qualifications is by studying at an approved school in the USA – but you will still have to take the Civil Aviation Authority exam when you return to the UK. You will also be expected to have flown a minimum of 1,500 hours and have gained experience on a modern flight guidance aircraft.

Obviously, we have only covered a few of the jobs related to transporting people from one place to another. Pass through any airport, major railway station or ferry terminal and you will see just how many people are involved in making these places run smoothly. If this is a part of the travel and tourism industry in which you are seriously interested, then start to explore the job market in a number of different areas. Tour operators offer a range of jobs related to transiting their customers. Airports have their own staff and so do handling agents, ferry and rail companies. Many jobs with these organisations will be advertised locally.

PROVIDING ACCOMMODATION AND SERVICES AT THE DESTINATION

The responsibilities of the tour operators don't end when they get their customers on to the aircraft. Travellers and holidaymakers who have chosen a package holiday expect to be looked after once they get to their destination. Depending on their own preferences and the service offered by their tour operator, they will expect to be met at the airport, taken to their hotel, given a welcome party, ferried around on excursions, entertained and provided with babysitters.

These are the jobs of the overseas staff employed (often on a temporary basis) by tour operators in the UK to spend the season working in holiday resorts.

Resort representatives

Resort representatives represent the tour operator at the holiday resort. They have a variety of duties, from welcoming holidaymakers on arrival to sorting out any crisis that might occur during their stay. They are expected to sell services, including trips and tours, to increase the tour operators' income.

They work and liaise with a wide cross-section of people, from holidaymakers (in their many and varied forms) to locals, officials and even the police.

Working conditions for resort representatives vary depending on the company they work for.

The work tends to be seasonal from May to October, or December to April if it is with a winter sports company. Many larger operators realise the value of hanging on to good resort staff and retain them throughout the winter months by offering training to work in head offices, travel agencies or alternative postings to winter resorts.

This is a very, very demanding job. Resort representatives are on call 24 hours a day, so they must be healthy, and have a lot of energy, stamina and patience. They also need:

- first-rate communications skills. They must be able to listen carefully to holidaymakers and to give information clearly
- knowledge of a foreign language, at least to conversational standard. Some tour operators are prepared to recruit people who do not have a second language, as long as they show a willingness to learn the local language
- basic literacy and numeracy skills as they have to organise and sell excursions and to keep simple accounts. In smaller resorts they may also sell foreign exchange
- a good sense of humour to deal with the guest who thinks their role is to join in the fun and get thrown in the swimming pool (fully clothed) with the rest of the gang.

Because of the nature of the work in resorts, companies often specify a minimum age (typically 20+). If you are under 20 but want to prepare for this type of work, get experience in customer service posts at home by waiting on tables in a restaurant, taking up retail work – anything that brings you into contact with the public. This is valuable experience to add to your CV.

Resort representatives may also be expected to have a specialist qualification. For example, winter sports representatives may be expected to have a skiing qualification, such as a minimum of BASI 3.

If you become a resort representative, you could be asked where you would like to work. Think very carefully. If there is a choice between the Maldives and the Costa del Sol, think about the skills and experience you have and how these relate to each resort. You may want to go to the Maldives, but your skills and experience may be more suited, and more valuable, to holidaymakers on the Costa del Sol.

As a resort representative you will be provided with accommodation. This will generally be fairly basic and will almost always involve sharing a room – one tour operator guarantees that its resort representatives will not have to share a room with more than six people!

Wages are not particularly high, hours are long and conditions can be gruelling. So why do so many people want this kind of work?

'Quite simply, I had great fun. I don't think I've ever worked so hard in my life and, in many ways, I wasn't experienced enough to deal with a lot of the customers, but I soon learned. It was a great way to work my way through the summer months, I met loads of really nice people and I had a great social life. It is difficult to resist the temptation to burn the candle at both ends. Because you are away from home, you shed a lot of the responsibilities that normally drag you down. And the sun shone every single day!'

Resort representative

MYTH BUSTER

Working as a resort representative, life is just one long holiday

It's not. As any resort representative will tell you, it is hard work that demands almost superhuman levels of tolerance and positive thinking. Once again we are back to the basic fact that holidaymakers have invested heavily in their holiday and they want it to be perfect. If it isn't, they want somebody to complain to. That somebody is the resort representative. Having said that, it is a good way to work overseas for a while and to build up a strong customer service skills base.

Tour guides/couriers

Tour guides and couriers travel with holidaymakers who have decided to take a holiday touring through a country or across a continent. They represent the tour operator to the holidaymakers and their main role is to make sure that everything runs efficiently.

The main duties of a tour guide or courier are to:

- check and confirm all travel arrangements en route
- ensure smooth transitions from different forms of transport and through borders and customs
- assign people to rooms as they arrive at hotels
- provide useful background information on local places of interest
- organise excursions or special events as requested by holidaymakers.

Tour guides and couriers work with holidaymakers 24 hours a day so they must enjoy working with a wide variety of people, be able to think on their feet, solve problems, be calm and polite at all times – and often they must be fluent in at least one foreign language. Communication skills and organisational abilities are key to success in this field.

'One of my most vivid memories of my experience as a tour guide is sitting on the steps of a hotel in Florence trying to get a party of 110 people into 88 beds, whilst the wiring in the restaurant caught fire! And, of course, there was a conference on at the time so every other hotel in Florence was fully booked.'

Tour guide

There are dozens of other jobs overseas that you could consider. Here we look at what a few of them entail and what criteria the recruiters search for in new staff.

Chalet person

Fancy a season's free skiing and a few weeks as a guest at one long house party? Think again. Working in a chalet can be one of the hardest jobs in a resort. Chalet staff are responsible for the smooth running of a chalet, including all the cleaning and cooking. In addition, they may have to live in the chalet so they must be able to get on with all types of people. Ideal candidates will be at least 21 or 22 years old. A cooking course/diploma and a great deal of experience of cooking for at least ten people is essential, as is the willingness and ability to do the housework.

Childcare manager/nanny

Many companies recruit childcare managers and teams of nannies. Their role is to keep children safe and entertained throughout their holiday. 'Children' can be aged anything from four months to 17 years and the sort of care you provide could range from changing nappies to organising sports for bored adolescents.

Looking after children carries with it huge responsibility, so maturity is important and some companies specify a minimum age of 24; others will demand that you are at least 19 years old. Responsible companies will expect childcare staff to have a relevant qualification, such as NNEB or equivalent, and extensive nannying experience. Evidence of crèche or nursery management experience is often required, and you will need good general management and organisational abilities.

Bar and restaurant staff

There are many vacancies for casual staff in resorts, either as waiters or bar staff. These roles can help you to build up customer care skills. Companies tend to look for bar staff with considerable experience, good organisational skills and good financial management. Again, many companies will only recruit bar staff aged 20 years or more. A bar manager will be expected to manage all aspects of a bar, including cash and stock control, bar presentation, marketing and staff management. Most companies will ask for evidence of bar management experience and/or relevant qualifications.

Chef

In any resort there will be a number of vacancies for qualified chefs. Head chefs will be responsible for staff management, maintaining accurate accounts, menu planning, ordering, stocktaking and budget control. Companies will be looking for maturity and certain professional qualifications – City and Guilds 706 1, 2 or advanced. Previous experience in the role will be essential. Other chef positions, such as sous chef, chef de partie and commis chef, all require City and Guilds 706 1+2 and experience of working in a large kitchen.

Waterfront manager

A waterfront manager manages waterfront staff, watersports equipment and organises programmes for instruction for holidaymakers. As with all management positions, companies are looking for maturity (age 21+) and experience. You will also need instructors' qualifications, such as those administered by the Royal Yachting Association and the British Water Ski Federation.

Often you will be expected to have instructors' qualifications in more than one sport, considerable instructing experience and, in case of mishap, first aid qualifications.

So if you think you'll apply to be a waterfront manager because you like sailing and waterskiing, think very carefully about the real skills and qualifications you can offer. You'll need much more than a good tan and muscles.

Tourist information centre staff

Another resort-based job is a tourist information assistant. In the UK you can find tourist information centres in all sorts of places: town centres, ports, railway stations, even council offices. Although they vary in size, they all serve the same basic purpose: to encourage tourists to visit an area and to answer any queries they may have. This could range from giving information on the local bus service to finding hotel accommodation anywhere in the country.

Tourist information centre assistants mainly deal with enquiries by post, telephone or from people visiting the centres. They provide information on places of interest, such as museums, historic buildings and stately homes. They also give out information on local travel and leisure facilities, such as theatres, cinemas, restaurants, sporting facilities. Tourist information centres hold information on the local area within a 50-mile radius. Having a good knowledge of local and national tourist attractions is a help, as is a grasp of national and local geography.

Successful tourist information centre assistants enjoy working with the public and can stay calm and polite when under pressure. Good communication skills are paramount, particularly the ability to listen so that you can find out exactly what a customer is looking for. Attention to detail and accuracy are also extremely important, especially when making reservations.

'I'm expected to know everything – the opening times of every attraction within 50 miles of here, what the weather will be like next Tuesday and where they left their shopping because now they can't find it. Most people are polite but you do get the odd awkward customer, like the ones who come to book accommodation at 5pm on a bank holiday weekend when you know there isn't an empty bed anywhere in the district.'

Tourist information centre manager

It is increasingly important for tourist information centre assistants to be computer literate. Many tourist information centres have websites so that visitors can find out about an area before they visit.

VITAL STATISTICS

Salaries

Starting salaries in the travel and tourism industry can be low, but there is often the potential to earn more by performance-related pay or commission on sales.

The following information should be taken as a broad guide only:

Travel agencies

- travel adviser/consultant £5,000–£8,000.

Tour operators

- administrative assistant/clerical/sales staff salaries start at around £10,000
- for management roles, salaries start at around £16,000 and can be higher if you work for a multinational
- cabin crew will start on a salary of £8,000–£11,000
- pilots can earn from £30,000 to £60,000
- resort representatives will be paid a basic of £6,000–£8,000, but can increase earnings through commission on excursions, etc.
- tourist information office assistants earn £5,000–£10,000.

Recent minimum wage legislation will view a salary in total, so all commission and bonus payments will be included. As a result, basic starting salaries do not have to be increased if overall earnings meet the minimum payment conditions.

Benefits packages

For management and office-based staff in the UK, benefits packages will be fairly standard and can include a range of the following:

- approximately 15–25 days' holiday plus bank holidays
- uniforms (quite common in travel agencies)
- travel subsidies for staff in central London
- pension and health care schemes
- discounted travel.

For resort staff, conditions and 'perks' will vary according to where you are and which company you work for, but can include:

- insurance for your stay abroad
- flights to and from the resort at the beginning and end of the season
- uniforms
- free accommodation (although this could be fairly basic)
- subsidised food and drinks
- free lift passes and ski hire if you work for a winter sports company.

'We recruit staff from the end of the season (May) onwards. Salaries for office staff range from £10,000 for a clerical role to £33,000 for senior management. Office staff generally work 9am–5.30pm but the hours can be much longer in the period coming up to the start of the season in November. Resort staff get between 500 and 1000 francs per week paid locally. In addition, they get free accommodation and food, lift pass, skis and boots and jackets. All staff get bonuses if the company does well. Chalet staff work 7.30am to midday, and then 6pm to 10pm, six days a week.'
Administration manager, winter sports company

Some of the larger companies are now working with colleges to create tailored courses that produce recruits with the skills and qualifications they need. Employment is virtually guaranteed on successful completion of these courses, so it is worth contacting the larger tour operators direct to see if they sponsor such schemes.

And now an answer to the question that a lot of potential recruits to the industry really want to ask – am I going to get lots of free holidays?

One of the perks of working for a travel agency is the occasional chance to travel, expenses paid. Generally these will be 'educational' trips, linked to finding out more about the facilities tour operators offer to their customers. 'Educationals' can be very hard work with a busy itinerary and, realistically, you can only expect such a trip about once every couple of years. Nevertheless, they can be great fun. You may also be eligible for some discount on holidays – but this may be a relatively small percentage of the overall cost.

If you work for a tour operator in a resort then you will be working overseas. Remember that word 'work'. You will be based in a resort for the duration of the season. Staff who are employed permanently as resort representatives may move from country to country every year. As they build up their career with the tour operator, they could be given a choice as to where they want to go next, although this choice will be closely related to their skills, experience and suitability for the resort.

Management staff working in sales, marketing and operations may travel frequently, particularly if their responsibilities involve overseeing staff in resorts and checking out new accommodation and tourist developments.

'I can't deny that the travel is a major attraction in my job. I go overseas every month or so and I still get a buzz from each trip. But it is incredibly hard work. From the minute I get to the airport, I am monitoring the services we offer, checking the airline, the hotels and the level of service our staff are offering. Once I am at a resort, I am in meetings all day with hotel managers and resort administrators, and mingling with guests to get feedback from them. I might pack my swimsuit, but I very rarely get a chance to wear it! Yes, the travel is great but it is very tiring and plays havoc with my home life.'

Sales director, tour operator

In Part One of *The Insider Career Guide to Travel and Tourism* we have looked at just some of the jobs that exist in the industry. By necessity, we can only consider a few of the options – there are more.

The information we have given is general. All companies will have their own specifications for staff. To find out their precise requirements, write to the companies direct. Be very wary of companies that do not ask for any qualifications or offer training. Working in travel and tourism is demanding; responsible companies will make sure their staff have the maturity and qualifications to enable them to succeed and will offer them plenty of support and training to develop the skills they need.

In Part Two, we look at 'the person' and find out more about the personal qualities and skills which are essential for people who want to succeed in the travel and tourism industry.

part two   the person

the person

Introduction

Part One of *The Insider Career Guide to Travel and Tourism* introduced some of the jobs available, some of the skills you might need and the type of culture you can expect to find in the industry. Part two focuses on the type of people recruiters are looking for. In this section, we look at the particular skills and personal qualities that you will need to succeed. By the end of this section you will have a better idea if you are suited to the travel and tourism industry – and if it is suited to you.

The travel and tourism industry is so diverse that it is difficult to pinpoint one set of skills or one specific personality type as 'ideal'. Opportunities exist for many different types of people. This is increasingly true as many specialist holiday companies are looking at a host of different ideas for holiday businesses. Take, for example, the job of tour guide. Typically, tour guides need to be outgoing, confident and able to cope with periods of extreme pressure. But different types of holidays may demand more particular skills. For example:

- A tour guide taking a group of travellers across Africa by Jeep will need good survival skills. They may need to be able to cook, repair a vehicle and cope with predominantly young clients.
- A tour guide on a cultural cruise to Greece may be expected to have a comprehensive knowledge of the area, and to have the poise to deal with mature and well-informed clients.
- A tour guide at a Spanish hotel specialising in family holidays needs to be outgoing, good with children, able to respond rapidly to changing groups of tourists and not afraid to join in the fun.

These are broad generalisations, but they give some indication of the variety of skills holiday companies look for to service the needs of different customers.

Finding the best job/career for you is a complex process. It involves matching your skills, expertise and experience with the requirements of an employer. The best place to start is by taking a close look at yourself.

MARKETING YOURSELF

When marketing professionals look at a strategy for a product or business, they often start with a SWOT analysis, which evaluates strengths, weaknesses, opportunities and threats. This is a good starting point for anyone who is looking for a new career or looking to develop an existing one. By looking at your own strengths, weaknesses, opportunities and threats you will start to formulate a strategy for your career. Here is a typical example of what a SWOT analysis might look like.

Strengths	Weaknesses
Lots of retail experience	Limited experience of travel
Friendly, outgoing personality	German could be better
Five GCSEs	Not confident about my
Basic knowledge of German	presentation skills
Travelled across Europe	
Opportunities	**Threats**
Work experience in a shop (customer service)	Competition for posts
Friend who works for a travel company	Applicants with greater experience

Now carry out your own SWOT analysis by copying out the grid and filling in the categories with information about yourself. Through this exercise, you will discover your strengths; these are the points you can 'sell' at interview. It will also highlight the areas where you need to improve. Don't be afraid of your weaknesses; if you can identify them, you can take positive action to overcome them. For example, you could start working to improve that language. Given time and direction, you can turn weaknesses into strengths. If you ignore your weaknesses, they will not go away.

Opportunities to find out more, to gain experience of an industry or to network and make contacts are always useful. Threats can be identified and a strategy can be developed to overcome these. For example, by improving your job-seeking skills you can make your applications stand out from the rest. If you can anticipate threats, you will not be confronted by any nasty surprises.

The key to finding out if you are suited to a particular career is being honest about yourself. Think about your achievements, skills, your likes and dislikes. Think about your personality. Are you outgoing and independent? How do you react to different problems? How well do you cope with pressure? Do you have plenty of stamina? There is no point applying to be a representative on a camp site in the south of France if you enjoy your own company and hate living in a tent.

Getting advice

Carrying out a personal analysis is a complex business and in this book we can only provide you with a few simple guidelines. If you need more help there are lots of sources of information to help you. You can:

- **Talk to a careers adviser.** If you are still in full-time education, you may be able to get help from your university or college careers service. Local authorities also have career services and they are increasingly offering their services to a wide range of people, not just school leavers. Staff at your local job centre or careers service may be able to help
- **Contact a private careers consultant.** There is a growing army of career consultants, some of whom specialise in particular industries. Before you commit yourself to working with a consultant, find out the range of services they offer, their fees (they can be very expensive) and their success rate. Some of the best consultants offer comprehensive services where they

carry out an audit of your skills, attitudes and experience to highlight the areas in which you will be most likely to succeed. They may act as headhunters for particular industries and be able to point you towards specific job opportunities. Consultants may go as far as suggesting improvements in your personal presentation, by suggesting styles and colours of clothing that will make the greatest impact at interview. You can find out details of these organisations in careers literature, in newspaper advertisements (often on the jobs pages), in the *Yellow Pages* and on the Internet.

- **Look at careers literature.** Again, there are plenty of books available offering advice on specific job-seeking skills. Many of these include sections on self audit techniques which will help you carry out your SWOT analysis.

At this stage you might also want to carry out a careers analysis, where you look at what you want from a specific career. This does not have to be a detailed exercise but it could help you to focus on what you really want. It will also help you to prepare answers for application forms and interview questions.

What do you want?

What do you expect from a career? Different people want different things, depending on their personality, their economic and domestic situation, the attitudes towards work that they have grown up with. They may be looking for:

- financial rewards
- friendship and a social life
- a challenge
- rapid promotion and recognition
- variety and the opportunity to travel
- security
- personal development and a chance to further their education and skills base.

Make your own list of at least six things you expect from your job.

    1. ....

    2. ....

    3. ....

    4. ....

    5. ....

    6. ....

Now list three types of work that interest you. These could be specific career areas or more vague determiners, such as work that brings you into contact with new people, working with computers or using foreign languages.

    1. ....

    2. ....

    3. ....

Think about the things you definitely *don't* want to do. These could be specific jobs or more general statements such as not wanting to work in an office.

    1. ....

    2. ....

    3. ....

Look back at some of the jobs and the roles we described in Part One of *The Insider Career Guide to Travel and Tourism*. Do the things you want match up with the types of work you have read about? Can you identify any particular areas within the industry for which you are particularly suited? For example, if security, long-term employment and an above-average salary are important to you, should you be considering working as a resort representative?

Next look at the practicalities of working life. Whatever job you take in the travel and tourism industry, there will be certain situations that you encounter. Answer yes or no to the following questions to find out if you can deal with them.

		Yes	No
1.	Do you have good numeracy and literacy skills?	☐	☐
2.	Do you have good communication skills (this means listening as well as speaking)?	☐	☐
3.	Do you enjoy working with people?	☐	☐
4.	Are you able to think on your feet?	☐	☐
5.	Do you have good problem-solving skills?	☐	☐
6.	Do you stay calm under pressure?	☐	☐
7.	Can you work on your own initiative?	☐	☐
8.	Are you a team player?	☐	☐
9.	Do you speak a second language?	☐	☐
10.	Are you computer literate?	☐	☐

If you have answered 'yes' to seven or more of these questions, a career in the travel and tourism industry may be suitable for you.

Reality check

Before you go any further, carry out a 'reality check'. Working in the travel and tourism industry is not a free ticket to exciting times in glamorous places all over the world. It involves hard work, often for limited pay. You may spend most of your time in an office rather than on a beach. '*I want to travel*' is a reason often given for entering the industry, but this urge may not be enough to equip you for the reality of a lot of the jobs on offer.

JUST FOR FUN...

Try our quizzes purely for fun. The first, 'About you', is not a complex psychometric test designed to give you a deep insight into your character, but it will help you to focus on some of the skills recruiters look for in successful applicants. These skills are examined in greater detail later on in Part Two.

About you...

1. You are asked to make a five-minute presentation to a group of 20 people. Does this:

    a. fill you with dread. You would rather spend an evening in a snake pit than address a group of people
    b. fill you with dread, but you see it as an opportunity to develop your presentation skills
    c. present a challenge – you are really looking forward to it.

2. When you are introduced to a new group of people, you:

    a. chat to as many people as possible, trying to find out as much about them as you can
    b. look for people who are standing apart from the crowd and try to engage them in conversation
    c. stand apart from the crowd, hoping someone will come up to you and start a conversation.

3. After a long journey, you have just arrived at a Spanish hotel with your party of 50 American tourists. You are busy issuing room keys, when several tourists ask you a number of questions at once – 'Where is my room?', 'Where is the bathroom?', 'Do they speak English here?' Do you:

    a. answer as many questions as possible, politely and calmly with a smile
    b. snap, 'How should I know? I arrived here at the same time as you!'
    c. tell them you will answer all of their questions in a few minutes if they can just be patient for a little while longer.

4. What does teamwork mean to you?

    a. playing the game because you have to be seen to do so
    b. an essential part of work. You can achieve so much more working together

c. a myth. The best way to get on is to stab people in the back, steal all their good ideas and pass them off as your own.

5.   At the end of a very long day, your boss asks you to do some urgent paperwork, which is needed for the following morning. Do you feel:

a. depressed. So much for the glamour of the travel and tourism industry. All you seem to do is hammer a keyboard.
b. annoyed. Doesn't anyone realise you have a life outside of work?
c. enthusiastic. You realised that paperwork and long hours were part of the job before you started.

These are the answers you *should* have given if you have the right attitude to work in travel and tourism.

1b or c. Either response is fine. There are very few people who enjoy public speaking or addressing large groups of people, but if you are working with the public, particularly in a resort, you will probably be asked to make a presentation at some point. Practice makes perfect. There are very few naturally gifted public speakers, but the more opportunities you have to practise your skills the better you will become.

If you work on the business development side for a tour operator, you will be expected to make presentations as part of your job. What is important is your willingness to develop your communication skills.

'I organise welcome parties for each new group of holidaymakers the day after they arrive. There can be 30 or 40 people in the room, all keen to get on with having a good time and not necessarily wanting to listen to me. You have to get their attention and keep it – this is the point when we tell them about the tours and excursions and try to get some sales. The first few times, I was rigid with embarrassment but my presentation skills have improved enormously and now I enjoy it.'
Resort representative

2a or b. In most areas of the travel and tourism industry, staff have to be friendly, outgoing and confident. If you are working in a resort, part of your role will be to make holidaymakers feel welcome. You will have to be proactive and take care of them, not wait for them to take care of you. Good interpersonal skills are essential and worth practising and improving.

> 'It doesn't matter which area of the industry you work in, you have to inspire confidence in the customers so that they will trust you. In a travel agency that means making them understand that you genuinely want them to have a good holiday. In a resort it means that you have to make the approaches and ensure that everybody is happy.'
>
> *Trainer, tour operator*

3a or c (although the temptation, particularly if you are tired, is obviously b). Tour guides or couriers are often surrounded by chaos which is not of their own making, so they have to try to be as organised and polite as possible at all times. The smile, although this may develop into a fixed grin, is also very important.

> 'When holidaymakers get off a plane, they are tired and often a bit anxious. Getting them booked in and settled at the hotel is the first thing we have to do and, of course, it gets chaotic. Hotels, particularly the large ones, are coping with a massive throughput of residents. So sometimes rooms aren't quite ready, keys have gone walkabout, or people don't immediately get the room with the sea view. You have to deal with everyone's complaints at once, and that isn't easy.'
>
> *Resort representative*

4b. Teamwork is essential when working for head office, in a travel agency or as a resort representative or tour guide.

> 'One of the best teams I have ever worked with was a team of four tour guides. Each had their own particular strengths, ranging from skills in a particular language, experience of working with people, decision making, local knowledge and diplomacy. The team was so closely knit that there was no one leader, but each member knew when to take the lead and they were constantly supported by the other team members. Between us we dealt with criminal
>
> *continued overleaf ...*

> activity amongst the holidaymakers, theft from a tour guide, loss of passports, loss of luggage and illness – all in five different countries. It was hard work but great fun. If we hadn't been able to work as a team and support each other, we would never have survived the tour!'
>
> *Sales director, tour operator*

5c. Well, perhaps enthusiastic would be going a bit far, but if you are going to succeed in this industry you must be willing to do mundane, routine work, particularly at the beginning of your career. Obviously, travel agency staff are carrying out office-based functions, but tour representatives will also have some administrative tasks, too. Resort representatives may routinely be expected to sort out accounts for excursions or travel itineraries late in the evening, when they have returned from a full day's work with tourists.

> 'My job combines talking to the public with a lot of paperwork – but I knew that before I started. If we get really busy then sometimes I have to work late to clear my desk – but it's certainly no more demanding in that respect than any other job I've done.'
>
> *Assistant manager, travel agency*

So what do you know about travel and tourism?

Recruiters will look for evidence of genuine interest in the industry. You don't need to be an authority on geography or fluent in a dozen languages, but an awareness of the world outside your own front door is essential. Try our quiz.

1. The mer de glace is:
    a. a stand-offish French mother-in-law
    b. a famous glacier above Chamonix
    c. a mirror
    d. a dry ski slope in Doncaster.

2   A franc and a mark are:
    a. two chaps you met in the pub last night
    b. French and German currency
    c. symbols that you will find on pottery
    d. measures for glasses of brandy in Switzerland.

3. 'Do've il duomo?' means
   a. Where is the cathedral? (in Italian)
   b. Where is the restaurant? (in French)
   c. Where can I find a man? (in Greek)
   d. Where is my horse? (in Spanish)

4. Is a Michelin star
   a. recognition that a restaurant serves particularly good food?
   b. a symbol indicating the quality of a tyre?
   c. a reward for weight watchers?
   d. recognition that a restaurant has a very good wine cellar?

And the answers are...
   1b, 2b, 3a, 4a.

WHAT ARE EMPLOYERS LOOKING FOR?

Having looked at what you have to offer, now you need to look at the most sought-after skills and experience from the industry's point of view.

There are some basic skills which will be valued by most organisations operating in the travel and tourism industry.

Frontline staff

The skills and qualities which are particularly relevant to people who work directly with the public in travel agencies, tour operators, airports and ports, resorts and tourist information centres include:

- good communication skills (both verbal and written)
- strong selling and customer care skills
- basic numeracy
- computer literacy (increasingly important in all functions)
- languages (a definite asset, but not always essential)
- smart appearance, with a high standard of self presentation
- good organisational skills.

Personal qualities count for a lot. Remember that customers who are planning and going on holiday are focusing on a source of pleasure in their lives. The tour companies need to encourage this 'feelgood' factor so their staff have to be upbeat and positive. Nobody is going to get enthusiastic about paying out a couple of thousand pounds for a holiday in St Lucia if the person selling it to them makes it sound as exciting as a wet weekend in a windy seaside town.

> 'We look very closely at candidates for jobs to see if they have the right sort of personality for this kind of work. The bottom line is that character is more important than qualifications – we can train people in the necessary skills for the job but we can't make them cheerful optimists if they are basically pessimists.'
> *Recruitment manager, travel agency*

The qualities travel agencies and tour operators look for are:

- enthusiasm
- a genuine liking for people and willingness to be helpful
- efficiency
- self-confidence
- determination to succeed, particularly when under pressure.

These may seem fairly standard human qualities; after all, most people are positive and sunny when things are going well. The question you need to ask yourself if you are considering working in travel and tourism is could you maintain all these positive characteristics all the time when you are with your customers?

> 'You must have a professional approach, but at the same time you have to be friendly, and able to talk to people of all ages. You must also be reliable and responsible. People who are looking for a holiday have often worked all year to be able to afford it so they are spending hard-earned cash. You have a responsibility to help them find the type of holiday they are looking for.'
> *Assistant manager in a travel agency*

Management staff

Many companies in the travel and tourism industry promote from within. They prefer to encourage and advance their own staff rather than look externally to fill key positions. If you find that you enjoy working in the industry as a result of working for one or two seasons at a resort, you may consider furthering your career by applying for a head office post. Chains of travel agencies have head offices, and airports and ports operate as large companies so management posts are also available in these organisations.

As with many careers, promotion within an organisation means that your role will change, becoming strategic rather than hands on. Most management/strategic roles are office based so you will have less contact with holidaymakers. In terms of personal skills and characteristics, management roles demand:

- good organisational skills
- a detailed knowledge of the industry
- good administrative skills
- good business sense
- leadership/supervisory skills
- the ability to work well in a team.

Head office staff

Head office functions can demand specialist qualifications or knowledge such as accountancy, human resource management, employment law, marketing qualifications and an understanding of IT systems at a strategic level. This profile of a human resources adviser illustrates one particular head office role and shows how it is possible to work your way up from a junior position to take on a job with considerable responsibility.

'I began work on a two-year youth training scheme in personnel, working for four days, with one day release to attend college. When I applied I was asked to do an aptitude test and was then invited for interview. Whilst I was training, I went on a variety of temporary placements to gain experience in many different areas of the company.

The first permanent job I had was a clerical post in personnel working on recruitment. I progressed from personnel assistant to personnel co-ordinator to my present job as human resources adviser.

It's a very varied job. I monitor sickness and provide information on issues such as maternity leave and benefits. On the recruitment side, I write job descriptions, carry out aptitude and psychometric tests, draw up shortlists of candidates and take part in interviews. I also help with appraisals and staff development schemes.

There is always a lot happening so there is never time to get bored. I feel that I have developed a worthwhile career and gained a lot of specialist skills and knowledge. I don't know how many other companies offer this sort of rapid career progress for non-graduates.'

Human resources adviser

You can get a good indication of the type of people companies are hoping to recruit by looking at their advertisements and, even better, accessing their recruitment pages on the Internet.

'First and foremost, we are looking for people who can offer commitment, professionalism and commercial awareness. Although our customers appreciate the relaxed and informal way that our consultants operate, they also expect accurate information, sound advice and reliable service. Talking to potential customers about your travel experiences is an important part of the job, but matching people's requirements to the products best suited for them is the essence of it.

The working environment can be very demanding, requiring long hours, the flexibility to switch between branches, or between branch and telesales, and the ability to stay cool under pressure. Any previous experience of a busy sales environment is an advantage.

Sharing your travel experiences with customers is an important part of your role because it gives your recommendations authority. Ideally you will have travelled extensively in at least two continents (excluding Europe and North America). A good general knowledge of European and world geography is essential, and will be tested at interview.

We aim for cultural and ethnic diversity in our sales team and have many nationalities working for us, however you must have fluent written and spoken English and the legal right to work in the UK for at least two years.'

Extract from the STA Travel website

Some companies are very specific, listing qualifications and detailed requirements, whilst other smaller companies have a less formal approach.

The director of a small successful ski company which has been operating for more than 13 years described her approach to recruitment.

'We employ four members of staff in the office. They work in administration, sales, marketing and operations. First and foremost, our staff must be good skiers. They must also have a good telephone manner, office experience and be organised. We send all of our staff out to the resorts to look at chalets, and that gives them excellent product knowledge. They also receive a free skiing holiday for themselves and their family.

My main criterion for chalet staff is that I must like them! The qualities that help me to like them are that they must be good cooks, have strong personalities, be flexible, organised and mature, and be fluent in French. Everyone who works for the company must have at least 20 weeks' skiing experience, although we don't ask for specific skiing qualifications such as BASI. We like to promote from within so, ideally, resort managers will have at least one season's experience working for the company. Age is not important. Maturity, however, is important as is an enthusiasm for skiing. We have staff working for us whose ages range from 21 to 53.'

Director, tour operator

To summarise...

So, are you the right sort of person for the travel and tourism industry? If you are a bilingual accountant with excellent communication skills who enjoys water-skiing, alternative therapies, flower arranging, Tuscan cookery, photography and climbing in the Andes, you should have no problems making a successful career for yourself.

An exaggeration, but developing communication skills and good customer-care skills will stand you in good stead when you start applying to organisations in this industry. The key to getting on in travel and tourism is flexibility and knowing how to adapt your skills to the specific requirements of the thousands of companies that are looking for staff every year.

In Part Two of *The Insider Career Guide to Travel and Tourism*, you have focused on the skills and personal qualities successful recruits to the industry demonstrate. In the third and final section of the book, we look at:

- the practicalities of finding a job
- opportunities for development and promotion
- related careers for anyone who wants to move on from this industry.

part three   getting in, getting on… getting out

getting in, getting on... getting out

Introduction

By now you should be getting a clearer idea of some of the opportunities that exist in travel and tourism and whether this could be the right industry for you.

The third part of *The Insider Career Guide to Travel and Tourism* focuses on how you can:

- get into the industry
- build a career
- move into other fields of employment if you feel it is time for something new.

The job market in general is highly competitive, and travel and tourism is no exception. There are lots of enthusiastic, well-qualified people competing for a limited number of jobs. When you are applying for a job, it is important to stand out from the crowd from the start to make sure that you get past the initial selection stage and into an interview. A little inside knowledge will help you to prepare an application that will be noticed for all the right reasons.

If you are invited for an interview, you can improve your chances by knowing what the selectors are looking for. By following some simple advice you can upgrade your interview technique.

When you have found the opportunity you want, how do you begin to shape your career? What prospects are there for advancement within the enormous range of jobs that make up the travel and tourism industry? This section examines opportunities for training and development and follows some of the paths recruits have taken.

Finally, if you decide you want to move on to something

new, the skills and experience you have gained could prove invaluable in other industries. So where should you look next?

GETTING IN

Where do you start?

Whether you are still at school, college or university, or are hoping to make a career change into travel and tourism, you need to find out what jobs are on offer. There are various ways to go about this.

Advertisements: careers specialists argue that answering advertisements is not the most effective way of getting the job you want, but it is still the route many of us take. You can:

- search national and local newspapers for job advertisements. Local newspapers will advertise for clerical, administrative and junior management positions. National newspapers may carry advertisements for more senior positions or jobs at head offices and will advertise resort-based posts and seasonal work
- look at holiday brochures and advertisements to find contact names for organisations to whom you can make speculative approaches. Holiday brochures will give you an insight into the types of holidays different companies offer so you can choose the organisation whose interests match your own
- surf the Internet. Large organisations have websites that outline their services, profile their company structure and publicise job vacancies. Some websites go into a fair amount of detail about the type of recruits they are looking for and will offer advice on making an application.

Don't limit your job search to responding to advertisements; there are plenty of other avenues to explore.

Careers services: your local careers service should provide advice on job seeking. They can be particularly useful if you are leaving school and want to combine work with continuing your education. Ask about Modern Apprenticeships (there is more information about these on page 59) or any other combined work and training programmes.

Careers fairs: these may be sponsored by a local business agency (such as a Training Enterprise Council [TEC]/Local Enterprise Council [LEC]) or by a college or university. They give employers a platform to present their job opportunities or training schemes to potential applicants.

Public libraries: most libraries have a careers section which will provide literature on specific careers areas. Many also stock professional journals that are useful for finding out inside information about trends within the industry. You can use the library's photocopier and Internet facility for a small fee. At the time of writing, libraries are linking up with TEC websites to publicise training opportunities.

Job centres: local travel agencies and tour operators may advertise vacancies through the job centre, so it is worth registering with your local office.

Employment and recruitment agencies: you will find branches of these on most high streets. They will liaise between you and an employer who is seeking new staff and can be very useful if you are seeking part-time or temporary work.

Personal contacts: statistically, this is one of the best ways of getting a job. Spread the word that you are looking for a way into travel and tourism. Your friends have other friends and somewhere along the line you could make contact with staff already working in the industry who know of vacancies.

Speculative approaches: if you have identified a company that you want to work for, then write to them and send a copy of your CV. There is an element of luck in making a speculative approach at the right time to get a job, but even if there are no immediate vacancies the employer may be willing to keep your details on file for the future. Ask about training schemes and for advice on how you can build up your skills base to improve your chances of getting in.

Once you have identified an opportunity, the next step is to make an application.

Applying for a specific job

Unless you have powerful contacts, or your skills are so much in demand that you are headhunted, you will have to make a formal application for a job. In the early stages, this involves either completing an application form or submitting your curriculum vitae (CV) to the organisation you want to work for. If you pass the preselection stages and the selectors think you have the skills, qualifications and experience which they need, you will be called for an interview or asked to take part in an assessment centre.

Your application form, CV and covering letter are the first point of contact with prospective employers so it is important that you get them right. One job advertisement can stimulate hundreds of responses, most of which will be rejected almost immediately. Employers don't have the time or resources to interview everybody who wants to work for them so they will be ruthless in weeding out any applications that do not meet their selection criteria.

The Insider guide to completing application forms

- Take your time; you cannot expect to complete an application form well if you try to fill it in during a spare half hour.
- Photocopy the form and use the copy as a rough draft. Complete this in pencil before you even think about starting to complete the original.
- Read through all the questions before you start.
- Make sure you do exactly what you are asked to do. If the form tells you to list your education in chronological order, start with your secondary school and work up to your most recent college or university course. If it asks for details of past employment in reverse chronological order, start with your most recent job.
- Answer the questions honestly; don't make claims you cannot substantiate.
- Get your facts straight. Check dates, particularly of periods of education and employment and try not to leave any unexplained gaps.

- Always try to give evidence of your skills and achievements. Employers want to know what you have done and what you can do now, not what you *think* you can do. Give examples that link your skills and experience to the skills they are looking for.
- Check your spelling, grammar and punctuation. Better still, get somebody else to check them for you.
- Use black ink to complete the original form. It may be photocopied numerous times by the selectors and lilac, silver or green ink do not come through clearly. They don't look very professional either.
- Make sure you submit the form before the closing date.
- Keep a record of the date when you submitted your application, who and where you sent it to. If you don't hear anything after a couple of weeks, you should chase up your application.

The Insider guide to writing effective CVs

If an organisation doesn't have a standard application form, you will be asked to send in your CV. Think of this as your own personal marketing brochure. It needs to be concise and effective.

- Keep a record of any information that could be relevant to a job application. Use this as the basis of your CV.
- Always tailor your CV to the job you are applying for. Different employers are looking for different qualities in their staff and you should make sure your CV meets the needs of any job specification you receive.
- Follow the same advice as for application forms – give evidence to support any claims you make about your skills and experience.
- Keep your CV to a reasonable length; two pages of A4 paper should be sufficient. If it is much longer you may be including too much detail and/or irrelevant information.
- Print a draft copy and check the spelling, punctuation and grammar. Don't rely on your computer software to proofread for you.

- Use good quality white, unlined paper for the final copy.
- Print your CV or get somebody to print it for you. It must be letter quality from an inkjet/laser printer.

Explore different styles for your CV. If you are just leaving school, college or university, then a straightforward chronological account of your education and work experience, together with some information on your interests and any responsible positions you have held, will be sufficient. If you are changing jobs, you could use a different format which highlights your past job roles or focuses on your skills and technical expertise. Make sure you list your responsibilities and achievements.

There are dozens of good guides on the market that will help you to develop an effective CV. If you are not confident that your CV is as good as it could be, buying a book could be a useful investment, or you can choose from a selection in your local library.

The Insider guide to writing effective covering letters

It used to be customary to send a very brief covering letter with a CV or application form. Now the importance of this piece of correspondence has been recognised; this is the piece of paper that will make the recruiter want to read on and study your application. You don't need to produce a ten-page masterpiece, but you should produce a letter that grabs the reader's attention. Make sure the covering letter states:

- which job you are applying for
- where you heard about the vacancy (employers use this information to monitor the success of their recruitment campaign)
- why you think you are a suitable candidate for the job. This should be no more than a short paragraph highlighting areas of experience or relevant skills that you have mentioned in your CV or application form.

Your letter should also include a closing paragraph in which you invite further contact from the employer.

Again, follow the guide for producing a CV: use good quality white paper, and an inkjet or laser printer.

If, rather than responding to an advertised vacancy, you are sending out a speculative letter to an organisation, get a named contact before you start your correspondence. Ring the head office of the organisation and ask to be put in contact with the personnel or human resources department. When you get through to them, ask for the name of the person to whom you should write.

Try to get additional information about what they are looking for in new staff and how the company structures its selection process.

The Insider guide to performing well at interviews

If your CV or application form and covering letter produce the right results, you will be invited to attend an interview.

Interviews are a two-way process. They help the employer to find out if you are the best person for the job and they help you to decide if this is the job you want. Most people feel nervous before an interview; after all there is a lot at stake. If you are willing to spend some time preparing for the event, you can go a long way towards improving your interview skills. This will increase your confidence so that you present yourself more positively when you meet the selectors.

Here is a brief guide to good interview techniques. If you are just starting your career, or have not experienced many interviews, invest in a book about interview skills. There are plenty of good titles on the market which offer useful and detailed advice to help you improve the communication skills you will need when you talk to a prospective employer.

Before the interview:
- Take time and prepare as thoroughly as you can.
- If the organisation has supplied any recruitment literature, read it carefully. What does it tell you about the type of people who work there?
- Find out all you can about the organisation to which you are applying. Look at company brochures, market

reports and Internet websites and read up on their performance, structure and company mission.

- Research the vacancy or traineeship. What does the work involve? How will your experience and skills help you meet the demands of the job? Again, look carefully at the job description or outlines of the training scheme you hope to join.
- Find out what format the interview will take? Is it with one person or a panel? Do you have to take any tests? How long will the whole process take? If you don't know, ring up your contact to find out.
- Think about the questions you might be asked. Can you produce evidence to support any statements you make about what you can do? We can all claim to be good leaders; the selector will want to know about a particular time when you demonstrated your leadership skills.
- Think about the questions you want to ask. Remember, the interview is a time for you to collect information.
- Put yourself in the role of the interviewer. What would you like to find out about the person being interviewed?

During the interview:
- Wear appropriate clothes and check that you are well-groomed. Dressing for success may be a cliché, but your appearance is important and is something on which you will be judged.
- Be punctual. Give yourself plenty of time to cope with traffic and to find somewhere to park. If you are travelling by train, tube or bus, allow for delays (they *always* happen when you don't need them). If you have an early interview and have to travel some distance, think about travelling the night before and staying over.
- Communicate your confidence through your body language. Walk and sit with your shoulders back and your head held up. Look at people when you talk to them and they talk to you. Smile. Breathing slowly and deeply will help to keep the nerves at bay. Try not to fiddle with your hair or sit with your arms folded.

- Listen to the questions carefully and don't interrupt. How else will you find out what the selector wants to know? Take your time when you answer. Speak slowly and clearly.
- Give evidence, evidence and more evidence. Support every claim you make with facts. Describe your achievements by saying what you did and how.
- Be honest. Don't make claims about your talents that you cannot support.
- At the end of the interview you will be asked if you have any further questions, so it is useful to prepare some questions in advance.
- Find out what happens next. How long will you have to wait for the selector's decision?
- Make sure that you end the interview on a positive note. Thank the interviewer, shake hands and *smile!*

The Insider guide to performing well at assessment centres

An assessment centre is not a place but a process whereby employers can take a detailed look at prospective candidates to find out more about their skills and aptitudes and thus their suitability for a job. It is a thorough way of analysing candidates, favoured by large organisations and companies which regularly recruit managerial staff.

Assessment centres vary in format. You may be asked to participate in a one-day session or to spend two days at a residential assessment centre. You will find yourself in the company of a number of other candidates for the same job(s) and you will be expected to work with them on detailed, work-related exercises. You may find yourself working on a committee, taking part in a role play, giving a presentation, preparing a report or making constructions out of paper. You could also be asked to sit tests to assess your numeracy and verbal communication skills. Organisations will usually send you copies of sample test papers to look at beforehand.

Throughout the proceedings, you will be observed by trained assessors who will be looking for evidence of skills such as your ability to work in a team and motivate others, as well as organisational, leadership, communication and decision-making skills. You will probably still be observed during meals or at times when you think you are free to relax.

If you attend an assessment centre:

- be willing to take part, even if you think that some of the exercises are more appropriate for the schoolroom. These activities all have a purpose and the assessors know what they are looking for
- work with the rest of the group. Even though you may all be vying for the same job, on most occasions you will not gain points by being aggressively competitive. Teamwork is the buzzword of today's workplace
- don't take over and dominate your group. Be prepared to listen as well as talk
- enjoy yourself – assessment centres can be a lot of fun – but don't get carried away. Completing a two-day course with a hangover is difficult and assessors often save the most difficult tasks until last.

Work experience

If you are just about to start your career, then a period of work experience can be an invaluable way of finding out if you have chosen the right field of employment. Work experience has become an integral part of secondary school education; it not only allows students to find out more about different jobs, it also educates them in the harsh realities of working life. The need for some ready cash has encouraged many young people to take part-time and vacation work or to spend their gap year in full-time employment.

The travel and tourism industry is ideal for this type of experience, particularly in customer care/service roles. Tour operators regularly recruit resort representatives for their winter and summer seasons and this is a great way to get a 'taster' of the industry. If you don't want to work overseas, travel agencies and tour operators may need temporary staff for their peak booking times (January to March for summer holidays, and September to November for winter holidays).

Getting in as a non-graduate

Opportunities for school leavers at age 16 are limited, although you may find an opening as a trainee in a travel agency or with a tour operator. Vacancies are generally advertised locally in newspapers or in travel agency shop windows.

If you seriously want to follow a career in this industry, then it is worth exploring the opportunities for two-year Modern Apprenticeship schemes. These offer structured training together with the chance to gain recognised qualifications and on-job training. In the first year of the scheme you will work towards NVQ level 2. Successful completion of the first year usually leads to the offer of a full-time job and the opportunity to study for NVQ level 3.

A variety of NVQs are on offer to people working in the travel industry, including Travel Studies, Business Travel and Business Administration. Contact individual companies to find out about their Modern Apprenticeship schemes. Schemes start at different times of the year, so make sure you find out when companies accept applications and the starting dates for the various schemes.

When recruiting for Modern Apprenticeships, companies are looking for people who are bright, with a good general education and who are enthusiastic and interested in travel.

Many colleges of further education offer GNVQs in Leisure and Tourism. These provide worthwhile qualifications that will enhance your application to a travel agency or tour operator. GNVQs at foundation level offer:

- an overview of the industry
- customer service skills
- product knowledge
- teamwork
- presentation and display.

GNVQs are educational qualifications so they are not linked to a specific company and there is no guarantee of a job when you finish the course.

For people aged 18+, there is a variety of UK-based jobs within travel agencies and tour operators. Travel agencies recruit:

- travel advisers/consultants
- foreign exchange staff.

Educational qualifications tend not to be as important as good communication and organisational skills. Companies may ask for a minimum of five GCSEs including English and Maths. They will almost certainly look for evidence of:

- good numeracy and literacy skills
- computer literacy
- some customer service experience. This could be in another industry but you should have worked face to face with customers or in a telesales role.

Language skills are always useful. A working knowledge of French, Spanish or German will help your application. There is also a demand (particularly in customer service roles at travel centres such as air and sea ports) for skills in Asian and Eastern European languages.

At 18+, there are also opportunities to start a career in head office functions such as marketing, finance, personnel and training. These vacancies are advertised as they arise, in the trade press, in national and local newspapers or on the Internet. Again, successful applicants will have good communication skills, a good general education, and a genuine interest in the travel industry.

Resort staff usually have to be 20 years of age or over. Again, academic qualifications are not as important as an appropriate skills base, although for specialist posts (such as a nanny or cook) they must have the relevant qualifications. Recruiters are looking for people who are outgoing, fun, practical, good communicators, mature and who have lots of energy and even more patience.

Many people apply to work in a resort for a season, but it can be a great first step in a career in travel and tourism. Companies are keen to keep good staff and will actively encourage good resort staff to apply for head office positions.

Getting in as a graduate

An increasing number of students are following courses in travel and tourism to degree or diploma level. You could study for an HNC/D in Travel and Tourism Management or explore a range of degree courses in International Travel and Tourism.

Whether you graduate in a travel and tourism-related subject or in another discipline (business studies or languages are particularly useful), you would be eligible for a place on a graduate training programme with one of the larger tour operators.

Competition for places on graduate training programmes in any large organisation is fierce and the travel and tourism industry is no exception. Graduates will be expected to have a good degree (2:1) and to show evidence of:

- leadership potential
- self-confidence
- effective communication skills
- business awareness
- teamworking
- problem-solving ability
- decision-making ability
- a willingness to take responsibility.

The recruitment process, as for any graduate training programme, will be thorough. Application forms will ask the usual questions about your education and work experience, but in addition you will be asked to complete more detailed sections. The questions may vary but you can anticipate some which ask you to demonstrate personal skills, such as:

- Describe a situation where you have shown, leadership/ teamworking/organisational/motivational skills.
- Describe a project in which you have been involved.

- Describe a difficult situation you have had to deal with.
- Describe a situation in which you have had to persuade other people to accept your views.

If you make it through the application form stage, anticipate at least one interview and an assessment centre. Companies invest a lot of money in training their future managers so they have to be sure they recruit the right people who will make a worthwhile contribution to their operation.

Some of the bigger organisations in the industry actively recruit graduates through the 'milk round' careers fairs at universities. Otherwise you will need to make direct approaches to the companies that interest you to find out what their graduate recruitment policy is.

The travel and tourism industry is a good career choice for women, with many of the larger companies employing far more (up to 80% of the workforce!) women than men at all levels. The regular hours and potential for working part-time or shifts in travel agencies and tour operators' call centres offer hundreds of opportunities for women returning to work. Increasingly, women are progressing into senior management roles.

GETTING ON

Prospects for promotion and advancement in the travel and tourism industry are generally good. Companies want staff who have a thorough grounding in the industry and the right sort of temperament to work in a demanding customer service environment. Consequently, they make the most of the people they recruit.

If you are willing to start your career in a relatively junior role, to take on any necessary training and to move to different locations, then you could make progress. As with most jobs, your prospects for promotion are ultimately dependent on your ability and performance.

In a travel agency, the assistant manager's role is an important first step on the management ladder. Successful assistant managers help to set the standard of service in a

MYTH BUSTER

The travel industry is only for young people

Yes, travel and tourism attracts large numbers of young applicants, partly because some office-based jobs are given to people with relatively low academic qualifications and little work experience. And yes, the demands of resort jobs mean that these jobs need people with a lot of energy, physical stamina and enthusiasm.

But large tour operators see the advantages of employing more mature staff, who have the poise and common sense to deal with people who are away from home. As long as you can show that you have the right outlook and the physical endurance to meet the needs of the job you apply for, age should not be an issue.

Travel agents also recruit across a wide age range. If the majority of staff you see working in this area seem young, that might have more to do with the salary levels than any form of discrimination on the part of employers.

travel agency, develop the team and deputise for the manager. Promotion can lead to a manager's job and then, within a larger group, to an area management or head office position.

If you have started your career in travel and tourism working in a resort, there are many possibilities open to you. If you believe that work in the travel and tourism industry is short-term, something to do for a season or two when you leave full-time education, but not a career — think again. Companies are always keen to retain and train good staff. As we have already said, many organisations retain good resort staff by offering office-based posts through the winter, or posts in winter resorts. Training is given to make sure staff have the relevant skills. After working in a resort, there is also the possibility of a head office management career.

Vacancies within organisations are often advertised internally. It is much more cost effective to promote someone from within an organisation than to look outside.

If you are ambitious and keen to succeed in your career, read any staff bulletins carefully. Also be willing to take on as much training as you can to develop your skills. It is up to you to make it clear that you are looking for a long-term career. Talk to your line manager about the opportunities that could be open to you. Some organisations offer staff the opportunity to change career path. For instance, some airlines run schemes that enable cabin crew to train as pilots.

> 'I started in telesales with a holiday booking company. The work was routine but the opportunities for promotion were good.
>
> During quiet periods of the year when fewer reservations were being made, we were "hired out" to other departments to help in their work. I spent a couple of weeks in marketing helping to prepare brochures and some time in the accounts department. It helped me to get a clearer picture of the way the organisation operates as a whole and, of course, it looks great on my appraisal form. After eight months with the company, they advertised a vacancy in marketing – and I got it.'
>
> *Marketing executive, tour operator*

Graduates who enter management trainee programmes will find themselves on structured courses designed to give them the broadest experience and training in a relatively short period. Companies in travel and tourism are keen to help potential managers develop both their personal skills (communication, decision-making and leadership skills) and their technical expertise (knowledge of markets, operations, accounting, IT, etc.).

Training programmes can last up to two years. They are constantly evolving in style and content but you can expect some of the following experiences:

- induction training
- modular courses to improve specific areas of knowledge and expertise
- placements.

GETTING OUT

Perhaps you have been working in travel and tourism for a long period of time and feel that it is time for something different?

Or maybe you have gone as far as you can with a particular company – a problem that can arise if you work up to the position of manager with a travel agency. What direction should you take next?

> 'The problem is not knowing where to go next...
> I'm happy with the company I work for, but now I'm the manager there's nowhere else for me to go. Head office is in another part of the country and for family reasons I can't relocate. The competition for regional management posts is really strong – there are a lot of managers like me competing for very few promotions. So I do feel a bit stuck unless I look for opportunities in another industry.'
>
> *Manager, travel agency*

People who succeed in travel and tourism develop a range of excellent skills that are transferable to almost any other industry.

> 'After three years in a busy travel agency, I think I've built up a fairly strong skills base. This place gives you excellent customer service training and I've also gained a lot of confidence in my IT skills and learned a lot about managing teams of staff. These are skills I could use almost anywhere.'
>
> *Assistant manager, travel agency*

Working in a travel agency provides good retail training and a basic grounding in retail management, so an obvious area to explore is retail management with another organisation. Employers will look for a good skills base rather than product knowledge; if you can sell holidays, you can probably sell fast-moving consumer goods. (You might want to look at *The Insider Career Guide to Retailing*, which looks at a variety of careers in this industry.)

Working in a resort builds good people skills, decision-making and problem-solving abilities – all of which can be put to good use in any customer service role. Your maturity and ability to stand on your own two feet have been proven by the fact that you worked abroad.

Your next step could be management training with a customer-focused function of an organisation.

> 'I've considered a number of sectors including customer liaison with a water company and personnel work with a manufacturing organisation. I'm confident that I could contribute to both because of the range of experience I've had working in a resort.'
>
> *Resort representative*

Other areas you might like to consider, which will use your interpersonal and communication skills, include:

- human resources management
- training
- sales and marketing
- telesales.

For many people, however, getting out isn't something they would seriously consider. In this expanding industry there are plenty of opportunities at all levels to make an interesting career. And, as many staff will tell you, it is an industry that can give its employees, as well as its consumers, a great deal of pleasure.

> 'Given the choice between selling and arranging holidays and selling shoes or cars, I know which I would prefer. It might sound a bit twee, but I get great satisfaction from helping other people to enjoy themselves. Most of them do – we have a regular stream of customers coming into the office after they get back from their holidays just to say thank you. What more can you ask for?'
>
> *Assistant manager, travel agency*

JARGON BUSTER

Travel and tourism, like all other industries, has its own special language. Here are a few of the terms you might come across when you start exploring careers in this area.

Administration
The management and organisation of a business

Assessment centre
Part of the recruitment process consisting of one or two days of tests and exercises where candidates are asked to perform tasks they may encounter in a particular job

Balances
Money outstanding after a deposit on a holiday has been paid

BASI
British Association of Ski Instructors

BWF
British Water Ski Federation

Call centres
Centres for telesales run by tour operators

Commission
Payment made to salespeople in addition to basic salary. May be a percentage of the sales or profit they achieve

Customer services
Any business function that directly influences the customer

Frontline
Dealing face to face with the public

Human resources management
Management function that relates to recruitment, training, employment law, discipline

Independent company
Not allied to another organisation

Long haul
Long distance, in relation to flights, i.e. to the Far East, Australasia, USA

Multinational company
A large company or commercial organisation operating in more than one country

Short haul
Short distance flights, i.e. internal flights within a country or continent

SWOT analysis
A marketing tool, an examination of strengths, weaknesses, opportunities and threats

Telesales
Sales generated by telephone

Tour operator
These organisations provide holidays by putting together a range of transport, accommodation and hospitality services. They may sell holidays through a travel agent or direct to the public

Transfer
The journey from a port, airport, train station to holiday accommodation

Travel agent
A travel agent sells holidays on behalf of a tour operator.

WANT TO FIND OUT MORE?

If you are seriously considering a career in travel and tourism, you will want to contact some of the professional bodies and organisations that operate within the industry. They may be able to supply more careers information or background to this employment sector.

A polite written request for information usually produces effective results and will do much to increase your understanding of how your career could develop. Alternatively, try their websites.

Association of British Travel Agents
68-71 Newman Street
London W1P 4AH
Tel: 0171 637 2444
www.abtanet.com

English Tourist Board/British Tourist Authority
Thames Tower
Black's Road
London W6 9EL
Tel: 0181 846 9000
www.visitbritain.com

Guild of Registered Tourist Guides
The Guild House
52D Borough High Street
London SE1 1XN
Tel: 0171 403 1115
www.blue-badge.org.uk/guild

Hospitality Training Foundation
Third floor
International House
High Street
London W5 5DB
Tel: 0181 579 2400 or 0891 44 33 22 (premium rate call)
www.htf.org.uk

Institute of Sports and Recreation Management
Giffard House
36-38 Sherrard Street
Melton Mowbray
Leicestershire LE13 1XJ
Tel: 01664 565531
www.isrm.co.uk

Institute of Travel and Tourism
113 Victoria Street
St Albans
Hertfordshire AL1 3TJ
Tel: 01727 854395

The Travel Training Company (a subsidiary of ABTA)
The Cornerstone
The Broadway
Woking
Surrey GU21 5AR
Tel: 01483 727321

For careers literature and advice, contact:
Careers and Occupational Information Centre
4th Floor
Moorfoot
Sheffield S1 4PQ
Tel: 0114 259 4564

Association of Graduate Careers and Advisory Services
(AGCAS)
Prospect House
Booth Street East
Manchester M13 9EP
Tel: 0161 277 5200

WANT TO READ ALL ABOUT IT?

There are a number of other publications that you might want to read on careers in this area. These include:

J. Christopher Holloway, *The Business of Tourism*, Addison Wesley Longman, 1998.

Mark Hempstall, *Getting a Job in Travel and Tourism*, How to Books, 1998.

Donna Sharon and Joanne Summers, *Great Careers for People Interested in Travel and Tourism*, Kogan Page, 1997.

Paul Brunt, *Market Research in Travel and Tourism*, Butterworth Heinemann, 1997.

Pauline Horner, *The Travel Industry in Britain*, Stanley Thomas, 1991.

Many companies operating in the travel and tourism industry produce their own literature. Write to individual companies to find out if they have recruitment guides.

Notes

The Insider Career Guides

Banking and the City
Karen Holmes
ISBN 1 85835 583 4

The Environment
Melanie Allen
ISBN 1 85835 588 5

Information and Communications Technology
Jacquetta Megarry
ISBN 1 85835 593 1

Retailing
Liz Edwards
ISBN 1 85835 578 8

Sport
Robin Hardwick
ISBN 1 85835 573 7

Travel and Tourism
Karen France
ISBN 1 85835 598 2

New titles
Watch out for three new insider guides coming out later in 1999 – the insider guide to successful job search (1 85835 815 9), the insider guide to interviews and other selection methods (1 85835 820 5), and the insider guide to networking (1 85835 825 6).

These and other Industrial Society titles are available from all good bookshops or direct from The Industrial Society on telephone 0870 400 1000 (p&p charges apply).